# Fingerprints
# of God

## Melanie Burgess

WestBow Press books may be ordered through booksellers or by contacting:

WestBow Press
A Division of Thomas Nelson & Zondervan
1663 Liberty Drive
Bloomington, IN 47403
www.westbowpress.com
844-714-3454

Because of the dynamic nature of the Internet, any web addresses or links contained in this book may have changed since publication and may no longer be valid. The views expressed in this work are solely those of the author and do not necessarily reflect the views of the publisher, and the publisher hereby disclaims any responsibility for them.

Any people depicted in stock imagery provided by Getty Images are models, and such images are being used for illustrative purposes only.
Certain stock imagery © Getty Images.

All Scripture marked with the designation "GW" is taken from GOD'S WORD®. © 1995, 2003, 2013, 2014, 2019, 2020 by God's Word to the Nations Mission Society. Used by permission.

Scripture marked (ICB) taken from the Holy Bible, International Children's Bible® Copyright© 1986, 1988, 1999, 2015 by Thomas Nelson. Used by permission. All rights reserved.

Scripture marked (KJV) taken from the King James Version of the Bible.

Scripture marked (Easy) taken from the HOLY BIBLE: EASY-TO-READ VERSION ©2014 by Bible League International. Used by permission.

ISBN: 978-1-6642-7172-2 (sc)
ISBN: 978-1-6642-7174-6 (hc)
ISBN: 978-1-6642-7173-9 (e)

Library of Congress Control Number: 2022912483

Print information available on the last page.

WestBow Press rev. date: 09/29/2022

WESTBOW
PRESS®
A DIVISION OF THOMAS NELSON
& ZONDERVAN

# Dedication

To my Mom and Dad. As I look back through the years, there are so many times I can clearly see God's fingerprints on you both! Thanks for always loving me! I love you both so much!

To Elsie May Morton, my little world changer! Let God's Fingerprints shine!!!

# Acknowledgements

**Andrew Wommack** founder of Andrew Wommack ministries and Charis Bible College for his teaching, *What's in your hand*. It was through listening to these teachings that faith arose in me to believe God for a creative idea.

**Romona Dutton and her handsome son Braedon Dutton** for allowing me to draw their beautiful faces.

# Thanks

I would like to thank God for giving me the ability to draw. Jesus for taking my sins in his own body, providing salvation for me and bringing me into a right relationship with God. And for the Holy Spirit that gave me the idea and words for this story. I love you so much!

If God had fingerprints where would they be? On the millions of stars overlooking a moonlit sea?

*Jeremiah 31:55 GW*

*The Lord provides the sun to be a light during the day. He orders the moon and stars to be lights during the night. He stirs up the sea so that its waves roar.*

# Are they painting a sunset at the end of a cool fall day?

*Psalm 65:8 GW*

*Those who live at the ends of the earth are in awe of your miraculous signs. The lands of the morning sunrise and evening sunset sing joyfully.*

Are they on the bear cubs as mama watches them play?

3

Can you see them on the poppies amidst the crimson fields?

How about on the wild horses? Would they be revealed?

If God had fingerprints where would they be? Do you think they would be very hard to see?

How hard would you really have to seek? Can you find them on the snow capped mountains of Pike's Peak?

**Are they on the wings of eagles spread wide as they soar?**

Job 39:27 GW

*Is it by your order that the eagle flies high and makes its nest on the heights?*

Are they found on the star fish,
washed along the sea shore?

If God had fingerprints where would you look? Can you find them on the screech owl sitting in a tree nook?

Do the katydids sing about
them late into the night?

**Can you find them on the rainbow, reflecting the colors of light?**

Genesis 9:13 ICB

*I am putting my rainbow in the clouds. It is the sign of the agreement between me and the earth.*

If God had fingerprints where would they be? Would you have to travel really far to see?

If you went out into the desert would you find God's fingerprints there?

If you looked really closely, are they on the prickly pear?

What about on a camel? Does he show off God's prints?

On the bearded dragon, or the scorpion, would you get a glimpse?

What if you traveled to a tropical rainforest, deep in the Amazon, would the howler monkey tell you what His prints are on?

Would he tell you to look on the glass frog, the toucan, or the giant river otter?

I bet he would tell you
God's fingerprints are
all over the Jesus lizard
as he runs on water.

How about we take a safari and travel through the African plains? Could we see God showing off His fingerprints all throughout the terrain?

What if you dove down deep
into the sea, and you came
across the blob fish, on him
would they be?

If you kept on swimming and came to the coral reef, would God's fingerprints be there, would then you have belief?

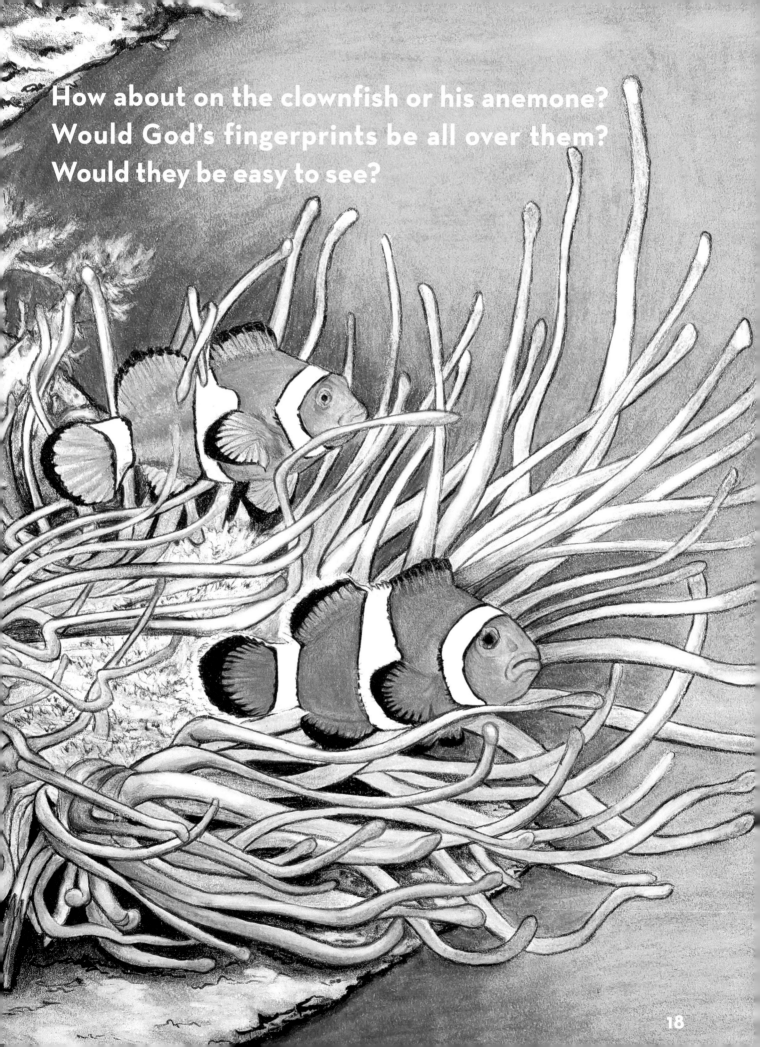

How about on the clownfish or his anemone?
Would God's fingerprints be all over them?
Would they be easy to see?

Suppose you went to Puerto Rico and visited Mosquito Bay. Would the glow of the bioluminescence be proof enough to say, "God's fingerprints are here. Look at this spectacular display!"

If God had fingerprints where would they be? How hard could they really be to see?

I think I know where you can find them. You can definitely see them, indeed!

Look on a monarch chrysalis hanging from the milkweed.

**On a peach, apple, raspberry, or pear. I can guarantee His fingerprints are there!**

*Mark 4:28 KJV*

*For the earth bringeth forth fruit of herself; first the blade, then the ear, after that the full corn in the ear.*

How about on a snowflake falling from the sky? Would the intricate detail be able to deny?

22

Do the leaves as they are changing
become filled with His prints?

Or the spring blossoms showing off, do their petals convince?

If God had fingerprints where would they be?
How hard would you have to look to see?

Are they on the spider in her web, glistening
from the morning dew?

# If we looked into a mirror could we see them on me, and on you?

*Genesis 1:27 KJV*

*So God created man in his own image, in the image of God created he him; male and female created he them.*

**Everything in creation reveals the fingerprints of God! Bursting forth with His glory, absolutely nothing is flawed!!**

**His fingerprints are everywhere showing off His awesome power! They scream of His magnificence hour after hour!**

*Romans 1:20 Easy*

*Ever since God made the world, he has been showing people clearly about himself. We cannot see God. But the things that he has made show us clearly what he is like. We can understand his great power that continues for ever. We can know that he is the true God. So there is no reason for anyone to say, 'We could not know about God.'*

**I'm so glad we decided to sit and have a look. If you stop and really think about it, God's fingerprints are even all over this book.**

*Colossians 1:16 KJV*

*for by him were all things created, that are in heaven, and that are in earth, visible and invisible, whether they be thrones, or dominions, or principalities, or powers: all things were created by him, and for him.*

# Fingerprint Fun Facts

- **Pikes Peak -** Pikes Peak is located in Pike National Forest, 12 miles west of downtown Colorado Springs, Colorado. The town of Manitou Springs lies at its base. Pikes Peak is the highest summit of the southern Front Range of the Rocky Mountains, in North America. Its elevation is 14,115.

- **Bald Eagles -** A bald eagle's wingspan is 6' for an average adult.

- **Starfish -** Starfish have no brain and no blood.

- **Screech Owl -** Screech owls are one of the smallest species of the owl. Their size is about the same as a robin.

- **Camel -** Camels do not store water in their humps. The humps store fat that the camel uses as nourishment when food is scarce.

- **Bearded Dragon -** Bearded dragons will wave at each other. Just like us, bearded dragons will wave when they see someone familiar.

- **Scorpion -** A scorpion will glow in UV light.

- **Glass Frog -** A glass frog can jump more than 10 feet in one jump.

- **The Jesus Lizard -** The Jesus lizard is a basilisk. They are referred to as a Jesus lizard because they run so fast they can run on top of the water.

- **Blobfish** - At their native depth, blobfish have a normal appearance. At the surface, without the water pressure to hold their shape, they transform into a blob-like appearance.

- **Coral Reef -** A coral reef is an underwater ecosystem characterized by reef-building corals. Corals are not plants. They are actually animals. They do not make their own food as plants do. Corals get their food from algae living in their tissues or by capturing and digesting prey. The algae, called zooxanthellae, is what gives the coral their beautiful array of colors.

- **The Clownfish and Sea Anenome** - The relationship between a sea anenome and a clown fish is interesting. Clownfish have a mucus-like substance on its layers that protect it from the anenome's sting. The clown fish keep the anenome clean and will hide in the tentacles of a sea anenome to protect it from its predators.

- **Bioluminescence** - Is when a living organism can produce light. It is common in squid, jellyfish, and plankton. Fireflies, or lightning bugs, are also bioluminescent.

- **Metamorphosis** - The process of transformation from a larva to an adult. There are 4 stages in the metamorphosis of a butterfly: egg, larva (caterpillar), pupa (chrysalis), and butterfly.

Printed in the United States
by Baker & Taylor Publisher Services